SHOPPING LIST

Yarn (Medium Weight)

MEDIUM 4

[7 ounces, 426 yards
(197 grams, 389 meters)
per skein**]**:

- ☐ Ecru - 1 skein
- ☐ Grey - 1 skein
- ☐ Rose - 1 skein

Crochet Hook

☐ Size J (6 mm)
or size needed for gauge

Additional Supplies

☐ Yarn needle

GAUGE INFORMATION

Each Motif = 6" (15.25 cm)
(from straight edge to straight edge)

Gauge Swatch:
3" (7.5 cm) diameter

Work same as Head Motif on page 4 through Rnd 2.

STITCH GUIDE

CLUSTER (uses one sp)

★ YO, insert hook in sp indicated, YO and pull up a loop, YO and draw through 2 loops on hook; repeat from ★ once **more**, YO and draw through all 3 loops on hook.

HEAD MOTIF (Make 8)

With Ecru, ch 6; join with slip st to form a ring.

Rnd 1 (Right side)**:** Ch 2 **(does not count as a st, now and throughout)**, dc in ring, ch 1, (work Cluster in ring, ch 1) 5 times; join with slip st to first dc: 6 ch-1 sps.

Note: Loop a short piece of yarn around any stitch to mark Rnd 1 as **right** side.

Rnd 2: Slip st in first ch-1 sp, ch 2, (dc, ch 1, work Cluster) in same sp, work (Cluster ch 1, Cluster) in next ch-1 sp and in each ch-1 sp around; join with slip st to first dc.

Rnd 3: Slip st in first ch-1 sp, ch 3 **(counts as first dc, now and throughout)**, 6 dc in same sp, 7 dc in next ch-1 sp and in each ch-1 sp around; join with slip st to first dc: 42 dc.

Rnd 4: Ch 1, sc in same st as joining and in next 6 dc, sc in sp **before** next dc ***(Fig. 3, page 44)***, ★ sc in next 7 dc, sc in sp **before** next dc; repeat from ★ around; join with slip st to first sc: 48 sc.

Rnd 5: Ch 3, dc in next 2 sc, (dc, ch 3, dc) in next sc, ★ dc in next 7 sc, (dc, ch 3, dc) in next sc; repeat from ★ around to last 4 sc, dc in last 4 sc; join with slip st to first dc, finish off: 54 dc.

EYE MOTIF (Make 2)

With Grey, ch 6; join with slip st to form a ring.

Rnd 1 (Right side)**:** Ch 2, dc in ring, ch 1, (work Cluster in ring, ch 1) 5 times; join with slip st to first dc, finish off: 6 ch-1 sps.

Note: Mark Rnd 1 as **right** side.

Rugs for Kids

Great for play areas and bedrooms, soft crochet rugs make fun decorative accessories for children's rooms. Each of Kristi Simpson's six designs is easy to crochet using colorful medium weight yarn.

Contents

LEISURE ARTS, INC.
Maumelle, Arkansas

OWL

EASY

Finished Size: 32" wide x 39" high (81.5 cm x 99 cm)

Rnd 2: With **right** side facing, join Rose with slip st in first ch-1 sp; ch 2, (dc, ch 1, work Cluster) in same sp, work (Cluster ch 1, Cluster) in next ch-1 sp and in each ch-1 sp around; join with slip st to first dc, finish off.

Rnd 3: With **right** side facing, join Ecru with dc in first ch-1 sp ***(see Joining With Dc, page 42)***; 6 dc in same sp, 7 dc in next ch-1 sp and in each ch-1 sp around; join with slip st to first dc: 42 dc.

Rnds 4 and 5: Repeat Rnds 4 and 5 of Head Motif: 54 dc.

BODY MOTIF (Make 10)

With Ecru, ch 6; join with slip st to form a ring.

Rnd 1 (Right side)**:** Ch 2, dc in ring, ch 1, (work Cluster in ring, ch 1) 5 times; join with slip st to first dc, finish off: 6 ch-1 sps.

Note: Mark Rnd 1 as **right** side.

Rnd 2: With **right** side facing, join Rose with slip st in first ch-1 sp; ch 2, (dc, ch 1, work Cluster) in same sp, work (Cluster ch 1, Cluster) in next ch-1 sp and in each ch-1 sp around; join with slip st to first dc.

Rnd 3: (Slip st, ch 3, 6 dc) in first ch-1 sp, 7 dc in next ch-1 sp and in each ch-1 sp around; join with slip st to first dc, finish off: 42 dc.

Rnd 4: With **right** side facing, join Grey with sc in same st as joining ***(see Joining With Sc, page 42)***; sc in next 6 dc, sc in sp **before** next dc, ★ sc in next 7 dc, sc in sp **before** next dc; repeat from ★ around; join with slip st to first sc, finish off: 48 sc.

Rnd 5: With **right** side facing, join Ecru with dc in same st as joining; dc in next 2 sc, (dc, ch 3, dc) in next sc, ★ dc in next 7 sc, (dc, ch 3, dc) in next sc; repeat from ★ around to last 4 sc, dc in last 4 sc; join with slip st to first dc, finish off: 54 dc.

WING MOTIF (Make 6)

With Grey, ch 6; join with slip st to form a ring.

Rnd 1 (Right side)**:** Ch 2, dc in ring, ch 1, (work Cluster in ring, ch 1) 5 times; join with slip st to first dc, finish off: 6 ch-1 sps.

Note: Mark Rnd 1 as **right** side.

Rnd 2: With **right** side facing, join Ecru with slip st in first ch-1 sp; ch 2, (dc, ch 1, work Cluster) in same sp, work (Cluster ch 1, Cluster) in next ch-1 sp and in each ch-1 sp around; join with slip st to first dc, finish off.

Rnd 3: (Slip st, ch 3, 6 dc) in first ch-1 sp, 7 dc in next ch-1 sp and in each ch-1 sp around; join with slip st to first dc, finish off: 42 dc.

Rnd 4: With **right** side facing, join Rose with sc in same st as joining; sc in next 6 dc, sc in sp **before** next dc, ★ sc in next 7 dc, sc in sp **before** next dc; repeat from ★ around; join with slip st to first sc, finish off: 48 sc.

Rnd 5: With **right** side facing, join Grey with dc in same st as joining; dc in next 2 sc, (dc, ch 3, dc) in next sc, ★ dc in next 7 sc, (dc, ch 3, dc) in next sc, repeat from ★ around to last 4 sc, dc in last 4 sc; join with slip st to first dc, finish off: 54 dc.

FINISHING

ASSEMBLY

Using Diagram as a guide for placement, sew Motifs together using Mattress St *(Figs. 4a & b, page 44)*.

Diagram

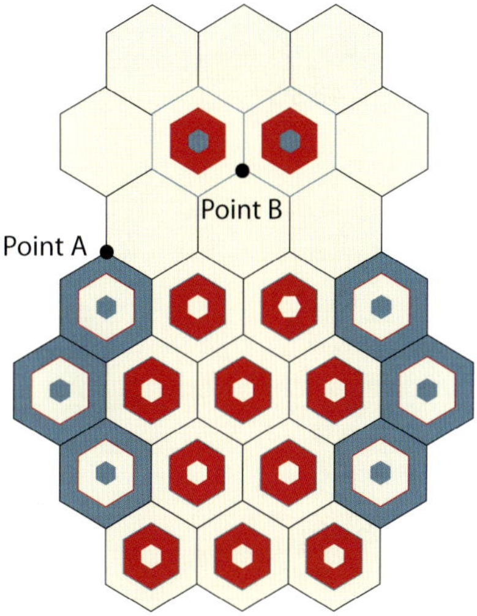

OUTER TRIM

With **wrong** side facing, join Ecru with slip st in ch at Point A; (ch 5, skip next st, slip st in next st) across to next Wing Motif, changing to Grey in last slip st made, (ch 5, skip next st, slip st in next st) across to next Body Motif, changing to Ecru in last slip st made, (ch 5, skip next st, slip st in next st) across to next Wing Motif, changing to Grey in last slip st made, (ch 5, skip next st, slip st in next st) across; join with slip st to joining slip st, finish off.

EYE TRIM

With **right** side facing, working in free loops of sts on both Eye Motifs *(Fig. 2a, page 43)*, join Grey with sc in dc at Point B; sc in each st around both Eye Motifs and between Eye Motifs; finish off.

BEAK

Using photo as a guide for placement and using satin stitch *(Figs. 8a & b, page 47)*, add Grey Beak to Head.

COW

Finished Size: 28" (71 cm) diameter

EASY

SHOPPING LIST

Yarn (Medium Weight)

MEDIUM 4

[7 ounces, 426 yards (197 grams, 389 meters) per skein**]**:

- ☐ White - 2 skeins
- ☐ Black - 60 yards (55 meters)
- ☐ Pink - 25 yards (23.5 meters)

Crochet Hook

- ☐ Size J (6 mm) **or** size needed for gauge

Additional Supplies

- ☐ Yarn needle

GAUGE INFORMATION

11 sc and 13 rows = 4" (10 cm);
11 dc = 4" (10 cm)

Gauge Swatch:
4½" (11.5 cm) diameter
With White, work same as Body through Rnd 3: 42 dc.

STITCH GUIDE

TREBLE CROCHET ***(abbreviated tr)***
YO twice, insert hook in st indicated, YO and pull up a loop (4 loops on hook), (YO and draw through 2 loops on hook) 3 times.

SINGLE CROCHET 2 TOGETHER ***(abbreviated sc2tog)***
Pull up a loop in each of next 2 sc, YO and draw through all 3 loops on hook **(counts as one sc)**.

BODY

With White, ch 7; join with slip st to form a ring.

Rnd 1 (Right side)**:** Ch 3 **(counts as first dc, now and throughout)**, 13 dc in ring; join with slip st to first dc: 14 dc.

Note: Loop a short piece of yarn around any stitch to mark Rnd 1 as **right** side.

Rnd 2: Ch 4 (**counts as first dc plus ch 1**), (dc in next dc, ch 1) around; join with slip st to first dc: 14 dc and 14 ch-1 sps.

Rnd 3: (Slip st, ch 3, 2 dc) in next ch-1 sp, 3 dc in next ch-1 sp and in each ch-1 sp around; join with slip st to first dc: 42 dc.

Rnd 4: Ch 1, (sc, hdc, dc) in same st as joining, ch 3, skip next 2 dc, ★ (sc, hdc, dc) in next dc, ch 3, skip next 2 dc; repeat from ★ around; join with slip st to first sc.

Rnd 5: Ch 1, slip st in next 2 sts and in next ch-3 sp, ★ ch 5, slip st in next ch-3 sp; repeat from ★ around, ch 2, dc in slip st at base of first ch-5 sp to form last ch-5 sp: 14 ch-5 sps.

Rnd 6: Ch 6, (slip st in next ch-5 sp, ch 6) around; join with slip st to dc at base of first ch-6.

Rnd 7: (Slip st, ch 3, 5 dc) in first ch-6 sp, 6 dc in next ch-6 sp and in each ch-6 sp around; join with slip st to first dc: 84 dc.

Rnds 8 and 9: Repeat Rnds 4 and 5: 28 ch-5 sps.

Rnd 10: (Ch 6, slip st in next ch-5 sp) around, ch 2, tr in dc at base of first ch-6 to form last ch-6 sp.

Rnd 11: Ch 1, (sc, hdc, dc) in last ch-6 sp made, ch 4, ★ (sc, hdc, dc) in next ch-6 sp, ch 4; repeat from ★ around; join with slip st to first sc: 84 sts and 28 ch-4 sps.

Rnd 12: Ch 1, slip st in next 2 sts and in next ch-4 sp, ★ ch 5, slip st in next ch-4 sp; repeat from ★ around, ch 2, dc in slip st at base of first ch-5 sp to form last ch-5 sp.

Rnd 13: Ch 5, (slip st in ch-5 sp, ch 5) around; join with slip st to dc at base of first ch-5.

Rnd 14: Ch 3, 5 dc in next ch-5 sp, (dc in next slip st, 5 dc in next ch-5 sp) around; join with slip st to first dc: 168 dc.

Rnds 15-21: Repeat Rnds 8-14: 336 dc.

Finish off.

HEAD

With White, ch 21.

Row 1 (Right side)**:** 2 Sc in second ch from hook, sc in each ch across to last ch, 2 sc in last ch: 22 sc.

Note: Mark Row 1 as **right** side.

Rows 2-4: Ch 1, turn; 2 sc in first sc, sc in each sc across to last sc, 2 sc in last sc: 28 sc.

Rows 5-23: Ch 1, turn; sc in each sc across.

Rows 24-29: Ch 1, turn; beginning in first sc, sc2tog, sc in each sc across to last 2 sc, sc2tog: 16 sc.

Trim: Ch 1, do **not** turn; sc in end of each row across to beginning ch; sc in free loop of each ch across ***(Fig. 2b, page 43)***; sc in end of each row across; slip st in first sc on Row 29, leave remaining sc unworked; finish off leaving a long end for sewing.

MUZZLE

With Pink, ch 18.

Row 1 (Right side)**:** Sc in second ch from hook and in each ch across: 17 sc.

Note: Mark Row 1 as **right** side.

Rows 2-4: Ch 1, turn; 2 sc in first sc, sc in each sc across to last sc, 2 sc in last sc: 23 sc.

Rows 5-8: Ch 1, turn; sc in each sc across.

Rows 9-11: Ch 1, turn; beginning in first sc, sc2tog, sc in each sc across to last 2 sc, sc2tog: 17 sc.

Finish off leaving a long end for sewing.

Using photo on page 13 as a guide for placement and straight stitch ***(Fig. 7, page 46)***, add Black "X" for nostrils. Using backstitch ***(Fig. 6, page 46)***, add Black mouth.

EYE (Make 2)

Rnd 1 (Right side)**:** With Black, ch 2, 6 sc in second ch from hook; join with slip st to first sc.

Note: Mark Rnd 1 as **right** side.

Rnd 2: Ch 1, 2 sc in same st as joining and in each sc around; join with slip st to first sc: 12 sc.

Rnd 3: Ch 1, sc in same st as joining, 2 sc in next sc, (sc in next sc, 2 sc in next sc) around; join with slip st to first sc: 18 sc.

Rnd 4: Ch 1, sc in same st as joining and in next sc, 2 sc in next sc, (sc in next 2 sc, 2 sc in next sc) around; join with slip st to first sc: 24 sc.

Rnd 5: Ch 1, sc in same st as joining and in next 2 sc, 2 sc in next sc, (sc in next 3 sc, 2 sc in next sc) around; join with slip st to first sc: 30 sc.

Rnd 6: Ch 1, sc in same st as joining and in next 3 sc, 2 sc in next sc, (sc in next 4 sc, 2 sc in next sc) around; join with slip st to first sc, finish off leaving a long end for sewing: 36 sc.

IRIS (Make 2)

Rnds 1-4: With White, work same as Eye: 24 sc.

Finish off leaving a long end for sewing.

PUPIL (Make 2)

Rnd 1 (Right side)**:** With Black, ch 2, 6 sc in second ch from hook; join with slip st to first sc.

Note: Mark Rnd 1 as **right** side.

Finish off leaving a long end for sewing.

EAR (Make 2)

Row 1: With White, ch 2, sc in second ch from hook.

Row 2 (Right side)**:** Ch 1, turn; 3 sc in sc.

Note: Mark Row 2 as **right** side.

Row 3: Ch 1, turn; 2 sc in first sc, sc in next sc, 2 sc in last sc: 5 sc.

Rows 4-8: Ch 1, turn; sc in each sc across.

Trim: Ch 1, do **not** turn; sc in end of each row across to beginning ch, 3 sc in free loop of ch at base of sc of Row 1; sc in end of each row across, slip st in first sc on Row 8, leave remaining sc unworked; finish off leaving a long end for sewing.

LEG (Make 4)

With Black, ch 11.

Row 1 (Right side)**:** Working in back ridge of beginning ch ***(Fig. 1, page 43)***, 2 sc in second ch from hook, sc in each ch across to last ch, 2 sc in last ch: 12 sc.

Note: Mark Row 1 as **right** side.

Row 2: Ch 3, turn; dc in first sc and in next 10 sc, 2 dc in last sc: 14 dc.

Rows 3 and 4: Ch 3, turn; dc in next dc and in each dc across.

Finish off.

Row 5: With **right** side facing, join White with dc in first dc ***(see Joining With Dc, page 42)***; dc in next dc and in each dc across.

Rows 6-11: Ch 3, turn; dc in next dc and in each dc across.

Finish off leaving a long end for sewing.

FINISHING

Using photo as a guide for placement, with **right** sides of all pieces facing and using long ends:

Sew Muzzle to bottom of Head.

Sew Pupils to Irises, then sew Irises to Eyes.

Sew Eyes and Ears to Head.

Sew Head and Legs to Body.

PENGUIN

EASY

Finished Size: 36" wide (from Wing to Wing) x 36" high (from Feet to top edge) (91.5 cm x 91.5 cm)

SHOPPING LIST

Yarn (Medium Weight)

MEDIUM 4

[7 ounces, 426 yards (197 grams, 389 meters) per skein]:

- ☐ White - 2 skeins
- ☐ Black - 130 yards (119 meters)
- ☐ Orange - 20 yards (18.5 meters)

Crochet Hook

- ☐ Size J (6 mm) **or** size needed for gauge

Additional Supplies

- ☐ Stitch markers
- ☐ Yarn needle

GAUGE INFORMATION

In pattern, 11 sts = 4" (10 cm);
Rows 1-8 = 3½" (9 cm)

Gauge Swatch:
4" wide x 3½" high
(10 cm x 9 cm)

With White, ch 12.

Row 1: Sc in second ch from hook and in each ch across: 11 sc.

Row 2: Ch 3 **(counts as first dc)**, turn; dc in next sc and in each sc across.

Row 3: Ch 1, turn; sc in each dc across.

Rows 4-8: Repeat Rows 2 and 3 twice, then repeat Row 2 once **more**.

Finish off.

STITCH GUIDE

SINGLE CROCHET 2 TOGETHER
(abbreviated sc2tog)

Pull up a loop in each of next 2 sts, YO and draw through all 3 loops on hook **(counts as one sc)**.

DOUBLE CROCHET 2 TOGETHER
(abbreviated dc2tog)
(uses next 2 sc)

★ YO, insert hook in **next** sc, YO and pull up a loop, YO and draw through 2 loops on hook; repeat from ★ once **more**, YO and draw through all 3 loops on hook **(counts as one dc)**.

BODY

With White, ch 70.

Row 1: Sc in second ch from hook and in each ch across: 69 sc.

Row 2 (Right side)**:** Ch 3 **(counts as first dc, now and throughout)**, turn; dc in first sc and in each sc across to last sc, 2 dc in last sc: 71 dc.

Note: Loop a short piece of yarn around any stitch to mark Row 2 as **right** side.

Row 3: Ch 1, turn; sc in each dc across.

Row 4: Ch 2 (**does not count as a st, now and throughout**), turn; dc in first sc and in each sc across.

Rows 5-44: Repeat Rows 3 and 4, 20 times.

Row 45 (Decrease row)**:** Ch 1, turn; sc in first dc, sc2tog, sc in each dc across to last 3 dc, sc2tog, sc in last dc: 69 sc.

Row 46 (Decrease row)**:** Ch 3, turn; dc2tog, dc in next sc and in each sc across to last 3 sc, dc2tog, dc in last sc: 67 dc.

Rows 47-64: Repeat Rows 45 and 46, 9 times: 31 dc.

Finish off.

EDGING

Rnd 1: With **right** side facing, join Black with sc in last dc on Row 64 *(see Joining With Sc, page 42)*; working in ends of rows, 2 sc in first dc row, sc in next sc row, (2 sc in next dc row. sc in next sc row) 9 times, sc in next dc row, place marker around sc just made for Right Wing placement, sc in same dc row and in next sc row, (2 sc in next dc row, sc in next sc row) across to beginning ch; working in free loops of beginning ch *(Fig. 2b, page 43)*, 3 sc in ch at base of first sc, sc in each ch across to last ch, 3 sc in last ch; working in ends of rows, sc in first sc row, (2 sc in next dc row, sc in next sc row) 15 times, sc in next dc row, place marker around sc just made for Left Wing placement, sc in same dc row, (sc in next sc row, 2 sc in next dc row) across; 2 sc in first dc on Row 64, sc in next 29 dc and in same st as first sc; join with slip st to first sc: 298 sc.

Rnd 2: Ch 2, do **not** turn; dc in same st as joining and in each sc around, moving each marker to new dc made and working 3 dc in center sc of each corner 3-sc group; join with slip st to first dc: 302 dc.

Rnd 3: Ch 1, sc in same st as joining, moving each marker to new sc made, (sc in each dc across to center dc of next corner 3-dc group, 3 sc in center dc) twice, sc in each dc across to last 31 dc, dc in last 31 dc; join with slip st to first sc: 306 sts.

Last Row: Ch 1, **turn**; sc in first 2 dc, hdc in next 2 dc, dc in next 23 dc, hdc in next 2 dc, sc in next 2 dc, slip st in next sc, leave remaining sts unworked; finish off.

RIGHT WING

Row 1: With **right** side facing, join Black with sc in marked sc for Right Wing; remove marker, sc in next 7 sc, hdc in next 4 sc, dc in next 8 sc: 20 sts.

Row 2: Ch 2, turn; dc in first 8 dc, hdc in next 4 hdc, sc in next 6 sc, sc2tog: 19 sts.

Row 3: Ch 1, turn; beginning in first sc, sc2tog, sc in next 5 sc, hdc in next 4 hdc, dc in last 8 dc: 18 sts.

Row 4: Ch 2, turn; dc in first 8 dc, hdc in next 4 hdc, sc in next 4 sc, sc2tog: 17 sts.

Row 5: Ch 1, turn; beginning in first sc, sc2tog, sc in next 3 sc, hdc in next 4 hdc, dc in last 8 dc; finish off: 16 sts.

LEFT WING

Row 1: With **right** side facing, join Black with slip st in marked sc for Left Wing; remove marker, ch 2, dc in same st as joining and in next 7 sc, hdc in next 4 sc, sc in next 8 sc: 20 sts.

Row 2: Ch 1, turn; beginning in first sc, sc2tog, sc in next 6 sc, hdc in next 4 hdc, dc in next 8 dc: 19 sts.

Row 3: Ch 2, turn; dc in first 8 dc, hdc in next 4 hdc, sc in next 5 sc, sc2tog: 18 sts.

Row 4: Ch 1, turn; beginning in first sc, sc2tog, sc in next 4 sc, hdc in next 4 hdc, dc in last 8 dc: 17 sts.

Row 5: Ch 2, turn; dc in first 8 dc, hdc in next 4 hdc, sc in next 3 sc, sc2tog; finish off: 16 sts.

TRIM

With **right** side facing, join Black with slip st in any st on last row of Edging; working from **left** to **right**, work reverse sc around entire piece ***(Figs. 5a-d, page 45)***; join with slip st to first st, finish off.

PEAK

Row 1 (Right side)**:** With Black, ch 2, sc in second ch from hook: one sc.

Note: Mark Row 1 as **right** side.

Row 2: Ch 1, turn; 3 sc in sc.

Row 3: Ch 1, turn; 3 sc in first sc, sc in next sc, 3 sc in last sc: 7 sc.

Row 4: Ch 1, turn; 2 sc in first sc, sc in next 5 sc, 2 sc in last sc: 9 sc.

Row 5: Ch 1, turn; sc in each sc across; finish off leaving a long end for sewing.

EYE (Make 2)

Rnd 1 (Right side)**:** With Black, ch 2, 6 sc in second ch from hook; join with slip st to first sc.

Note: Mark Rnd 1 as **right** side.

Rnd 2: Ch 1, 2 sc in same st as joining and in each sc around; join with slip st to first sc, finish off leaving a long end for sewing.

BEAK

Row 1 (Right side)**:** With Orange, ch 2, 2 sc in second ch from hook.

Note: Mark Row 1 as **right** side.

Row 2: Ch 1, turn; 2 sc in each sc across: 4 sc.

Row 3: Ch 1, turn; sc in each sc across; finish off leaving a long end for sewing.

FOOT (Make 2)

Row 1 (Right side)**:** With Orange, ch 4, 7 dc in fourth ch from hook **(3 skipped chs count as first dc)**; do **not** join: 8 dc.

Note: Mark Row 1 as **right** side.

Row 2: Ch 3 **(counts as first dc)**, turn; dc in first dc, 2 dc in next dc and in each dc across: 16 dc.

Row 3: Ch 3 **(counts as first dc)**, turn; 2 dc in next dc, ★ dc in next dc, 2 dc in next dc; repeat from ★ across; finish off: 24 dc.

FINISHING

Using photo as a guide for placement, with **right** sides of all pieces facing and using long ends:

Sew Peak to center top of Body.

Using satin stitch ***(Fig. 8b, page 47)***, add White to each Eye.

Sew Eyes to Body.

Sew Beak to Body.

Sew straight edge of Feet to bottom edge of Body behind Edging.

RACETRACK

Finished Size: 30" (76 cm) square

EASY

SHOPPING LIST

Yarn (Medium Weight) MEDIUM 4

[7 ounces, 426 yards
(197 grams, 389 meters)
per skein]:

- ☐ Green - 2 skeins
- ☐ Black - 1 skein
- ☐ Blue - 15 yards (13.5 meters)
- ☐ Yellow - 10 yards (9 meters)

Crochet Hook

- ☐ Size J (6 mm) **or** size needed for gauge

Additional Supplies

- ☐ Pins
- ☐ Yarn needle

GAUGE INFORMATION

11 dc = 4" (10 cm);
6 rows = 3½" (9 cm)

Gauge Swatch:
4" wide x 3½" high
(10 cm x 9 cm)

With Green, ch 13.

Row 1: Dc in fourth ch from hook **(3 skipped chs count as first dc)** and in each ch across: 11 dc.

Rows 2-6: Ch 3 **(counts as first dc)**, turn; dc in next dc and in each dc across.

Finish off.

SQUARE (Make 4)

With Green, ch 34, place marker in third ch from hook for st placement.

Row 1 (Wrong side)**:** Dc in fourth ch from hook and in each ch across **(3 skipped chs count as first dc, now and throughout)**: 32 sc.

Note: Loop a short piece of yarn around the **back** of any stitch on Row 1 to mark **right** side **and** bottom edge.

Rows 2-20: Ch 2 **(does not count as a st)**, turn; dc in first dc and in each dc across.

Trim: Ch 1, do **not** turn; † working in ends of rows, sc in first row, 2 sc in next row, (sc in next row, 2 sc in next row) across †; working in free loops of beginning ch ***(Fig. 2b, page 43)***, 3 sc in marked ch, sc in each ch across to last ch, 3 sc in last ch, repeat from † to † once; 3 sc in first dc, sc in each dc across to last dc, 3 sc in last dc; join with slip st to first sc, finish off: 132 sc.

ASSEMBLY

Hold two Squares side-by-side with **wrong** sides facing and bottom edges at same end. Thread yarn needle with Green and sew Squares together using Mattress St ***(Figs. 4a & b, page 44)*** beginning in center sc of first corner and ending in center sc of next corner. Join remaining two Squares together in same manner; then sew strips together.

OUTER ROAD

Rnd 1: With **right** side facing, join Black with dc in center sc of any corner 3-sc group ***(see Joining With Dc, page 42)***; 2 dc in same st, ★ dc in next sc and in each sc across to center sc of next corner 3-sc group, 3 dc in center sc; repeat from ★ 2 times **more**, dc in next sc and in each sc across; join with slip st to first dc.

Rnds 2-5: Ch 3 (**counts as first dc**), dc in next dc and in each dc around working 3 dc in center dc of each corner 3-dc group; join with slip st to first dc.

Finish off.

Rnd 6: With **right** side facing, join Green with slip st in any dc; working from **left** to **right**, work reverse sc in each dc around working 3 reverse sc in each corner ***(Figs. 5a-d, page 45)***; join with slip st to first st, finish off.

POND & ROAD

Rnd 1 (Right side)**:** With Blue, ch 3, 10 dc in third ch from hook; join with slip st to first dc: 10 dc.

Note: Mark Rnd 1 as **right** side.

Rnd 2: Ch 2 (**does not count as a st, now and throughout**), 2 dc in same st as joining and in each dc around; join with slip st to first dc: 20 dc.

Rnd 3: Ch 2, dc in same st as joining, 2 dc in next dc, (dc in next dc, dc in next 2 dc) around; join with slip st to first dc: 30 dc.

Rnd 4: Ch 2, dc in same st as joining and in next dc, 2 dc in next dc, (dc in next 2 dc, 2 dc in next dc) around; join with slip st to first dc, finish off: 40 dc.

Rnd 5: With **right** side facing and leaving a long end for sewing, join Black with slip st in same st as joining; ch 2, dc in same st and in next 2 dc, 2 dc in next dc, (dc in next 3 dc, 2 dc in next dc) around; join with slip st to first dc: 50 dc.

Rnd 6: Ch 2, dc in same st as joining and in next 3 dc, 2 dc in next dc, (dc in next 4 dc, 2 dc in next dc) around; join with slip st to first dc: 60 dc.

Rnd 7: Ch 2, dc in same st as joining and in next 4 dc, 2 dc in next dc, (dc in next 5 dc, 2 dc in next dc) around; join with slip st to first dc: 70 dc.

Rnd 8: Ch 2, dc in same st as joining and in next 5 dc, 2 dc in next dc, (dc in next 6 dc, 2 dc in next dc) around; join with slip st to first dc, do **not** finish off: 80 dc.

ROAD #1

Row 1: Ch 3 (**counts as first dc, now and throughout**), dc in next 7 dc, leave remaining dc unworked: 8 dc.

Rows 2-23: Ch 3, turn; dc in next dc and in each dc across.

Finish off leaving a long end for sewing.

ROAD #2

Row 1: With **right** side of Pond & Road facing and leaving a long end for sewing, skip next 12 dc from last dc on Row 1 of Road #1 and join Black with dc in next dc; dc in next 7 dc, leave remaining dc unworked: 8 dc.

Rows 2-23: Ch 3, turn; dc in next dc and in each dc across.

Finish off leaving a long end for sewing.

ROAD #3

With Black, ch 10.

Row 1 (Right side)**:** Dc in fourth ch from hook and in each ch across: 8 dc.

Rows 2-22: Ch 3, turn; dc in next dc and in each dc across.

Finish off leaving a long end for sewing.

ROAD #4

Work same as Road #3 for 17 rows.

Finish off leaving a long end for sewing.

FINISHING

Using Diagram as a guide for placement, pin Roads to Rug; then sew Roads in place with long ends.

Using photo as a guide for placement and running st ***(Fig. 9, page 47)***, add Yellow center lines to Roads.

Diagram

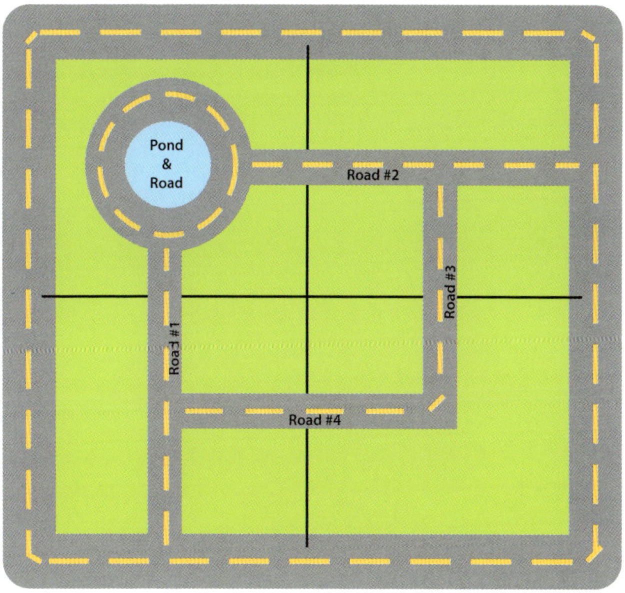

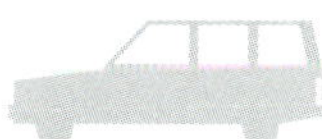

ROCKET

EASY

Finished Size: 22½" wide x 42" high (57 cm x 106.5 cm)

SHOPPING LIST

Yarn (Medium Weight) MEDIUM 4

[7 ounces, 426 yards (197 grams, 389 meters) per skein**]**:

- ☐ Blue - 1 skein
- ☐ Grey - 115 yards (105 meters)
- ☐ Orange - 75 yards (68.5 meters)
- ☐ Yellow - 20 yards (18.5 meters)

Crochet Hook

- ☐ Size J (6 mm) **or** size needed for gauge

Additional Supplies

- ☐ Yarn needle

GAUGE INFORMATION

In pattern, 11 sts = 4" (10 cm); Rows 1-8 = 3½" (9 cm)

Gauge Swatch:

4" wide x 3½" high (10 cm x 9 cm)

Ch 12.

Row 1: Sc in second ch from hook and in each ch across: 11 sc.

Row 2: Ch 3 **(counts as first dc)**, turn; dc in next sc and in each sc across.

Row 3: Ch 1, turn; sc in each dc across.

Rows 4-8: Repeat Rows 2 and 3 twice, then repeat Row 2 once **more**.

Finish off.

STITCH GUIDE

SINGLE CROCHET 2 TOGETHER

(abbreviated sc2tog)

Pull up a loop in each of next 2 sts, YO and draw through all 3 loops on hook **(counts as one sc)**.

DOUBLE CROCHET 2 TOGETHER

(abbreviated dc2tog)

(uses next 2 sc)

★ YO, insert hook in **next** sc, YO and pull up a loop, YO and draw through 2 loops on hook; repeat from ★ once **more**, YO and draw through all 3 loops on hook **(counts as one dc)**.

BODY

With Blue, ch 61; place marker in second ch from hook for Edging placement.

Row 1 (Right side)**:** Sc in back ridge of second ch from hook and each ch across ***(Fig. 1, page 43)***: 60 sc.

Note: Loop a short piece of yarn around any stitch to mark Row 1 as **right** side.

Row 2 (Decrease row)**:** Ch 3 **(counts as first dc, now and throughout)**, turn; dc2tog, dc in next sc and in each sc across to last 3 sc, dc2tog, dc in last sc: 58 dc.

Row 3: Ch 1, turn; sc in each dc across.

Rows 4-8: Repeat Rows 2 and 3 twice, then repeat Row 2 once **more**: 52 dc.

Row 9: Ch 1, turn; sc in each dc across.

Row 10: Ch 2 **(does not count as a st, now and throughout)**, turn; dc in first sc and in each sc across.

Rows 11-50: Repeat Rows 9 and 10, 20 times.

Row 51 (Decrease row)**:** Ch 1, turn; sc in first dc, sc2tog, sc in each dc across to last 3 dc, sc2tog, sc in last dc: 50 sc.

Row 52 (Decrease row)**:** Ch 3, turn; dc2tog, dc in next sc and in each sc across to last 3 sc, dc2tog, dc in last sc: 48 dc.

Rows 53-60: Repeat Rows 51 and 52, 4 times: 32 dc.

Finish off.

Row 61: With **right** side facing, join Grey with sc in first dc ***(see Joining With Sc, page 42)***; sc2tog, sc in each dc across to last 3 dc, sc2tog, sc in last dc: 30 sc.

Row 62 (Decrease row)**:** Ch 3, turn; dc2tog, dc in next sc and in each sc across to last 3 sc, dc2tog, dc in last sc; finish off: 28 dc.

Rows 63 and 64: With Blue, repeat Rows 61 and 62: 24 dc.

Rows 65 and 66: With Grey repeat Rows 61 and 62; do **not** finish off: 20 dc.

Rows 67-71: Repeat Rows 51 and 52 twice, then repeat Row 51 once **more**: 10 sc.

Row 72: Ch 3, turn; dc2tog twice, dc in next sc, dc2tog twice: 6 dc.

Row 73: Ch 1, turn; beginning in first dc, sc2tog across: 3 sc.

Row 74: Ch 2, turn; YO, insert hook in first sc, YO and pull up a loop, YO and draw through 2 loops on hook, ★ YO, insert hook in **next** sc, YO and pull up a loop, YO and draw through 2 loops on hook; repeat from ★ once **more**, YO and draw through all 4 loops on hook (**counts as one dc**); finish off.

EDGING

Rnd 1: With **right** side facing, join Blue with sc in free loop of marked ch ***(Fig. A)***; 2 sc in same ch; sc evenly across ends of rows to Row 74; 3 sc in dc; sc evenly across ends of rows to beginning ch; working in free loops of beginning ch, 3 sc in first ch, sc in each ch across; join with slip st to first sc, finish off.

Fig. A

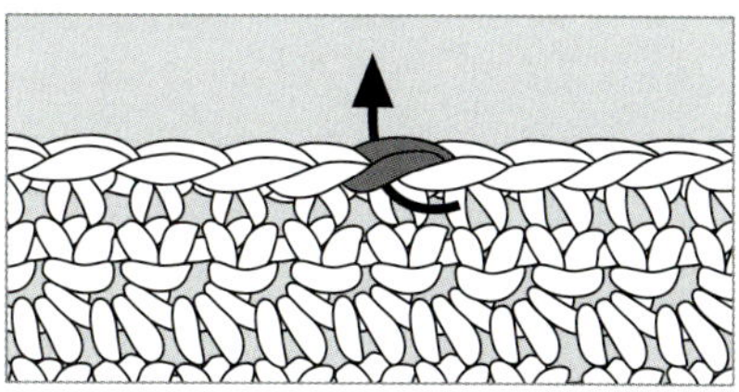

FLAME

With Orange and leaving a long end for sewing, ch 34.

Row 1 (Right side)**:** Working in back ridges of beginning ch, 2 sc in second ch from hook, sc in each ch across to last ch, 2 sc in last ch: 35 sc.

Note: Mark Row 1 as **right** side.

Row 2: Ch 3, turn; dc in next sc and in each sc across.

Row 3 (Increase row)**:** Ch 1, turn; 2 sc in first dc, sc in each dc across to last dc, 2 sc in last dc: 37 sc.

Rows 4-7: Repeat Rows 2 and 3 twice: 41 sc.

Row 8: Ch 3, turn; dc in first sc and in each sc across to last sc, 2 dc in last sc: 43 dc.

Row 9: Ch 1, turn; 2 sc in first dc, sc in each dc across to last dc, 2 sc in last dc: 45 sc.

Row 10 (Decrease row)**:** Turn; slip st in first 11 sc, ch 3, dc in next sc and in each sc across to last 10 sc, leave remaining sc unworked: 25 dc.

Row 11 (Increase row)**:** Ch 1, turn; 2 sc in first dc, sc in each dc across to last dc, 2 sc in last dc: 27 sc.

Row 12 (Increase row)**:** Ch 3, turn; dc in first sc and in each sc across to last sc, 2 dc in last sc: 29 dc.

Rows 13-15: Repeat Rows 11 and 12 once, then repeat Row 11 once **more**: 35 sc.

Rows 16-21: Repeat Rows 10-15: 25 sc.

Finish off.

Using photo as a guide for placement and long end, sew Flame to center of Rnd 1 of Edging at bottom of Body using Mattress St ***(Figs. 4a & b, page 44)***.

Trim: With **right** side facing, join Grey with slip st in first unworked sc on Rnd 1 of Edging before Flame, ch 1; working from **left** to **right**, work reverse sc in same st ***(Figs. 5a-d, page 45)*** and in each sc around working 3 reverse sc in each corner ending in last sc after Flame and changing to Orange in last reverse sc made on Body after Flame, work reverse sc in evenly around working 3 reverse sc in each corner; join with slip st to first st, finish off.

WINDOW (Make 2)

Rnd 1 (Right side)**:** With Yellow, ch 3, 10 dc in third ch from hook; join with slip st to first dc: 10 dc.

Note: Mark Rnd 1 as **right** side.

Rnd 2: Ch 2, 2 dc in same st as joining and in each dc around; join with slip st to first dc: 20 dc.

Rnd 3: Ch 1, sc in same st as joining, 2 sc in next dc, (sc in next dc, 2 sc in next dc) around; join with slip st to first sc, finish off: 30 sc.

Rnd 4: With **right** side facing, join Grey with slip st in any sc; ch 2, 2 dc in same st as joining, dc in next 2 sc, (2 dc in next sc, dc in next 2 sc) around; join with slip st to first dc: 40 dc.

Rnd 5: Ch 2, 2 dc in same st as joining, dc in next 3 dc, (2 dc in next dc, dc in next 3 dc) around; join with slip st to first dc: 50 dc.

Rnd 6: Ch 1, 2 sc in same st as joining, sc in next 4 dc, 2 sc in next dc, (sc in next 4 dc, 2 sc in next dc) around; join with slip st to first sc, finish off leaving a long end for sewing: 60 sc.

Using photo as a guide for placement and long ends, sew Windows to Body.

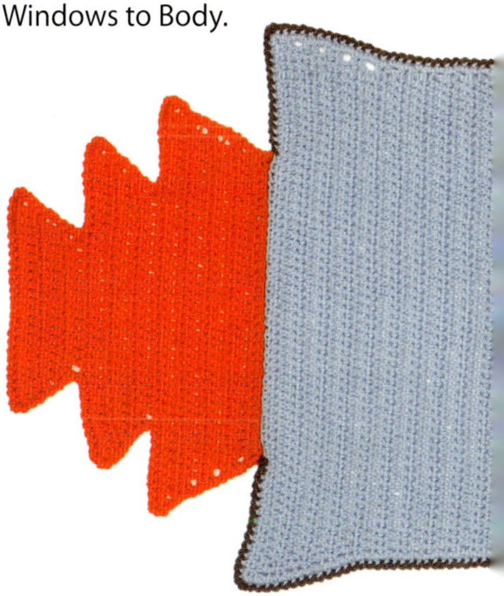

UNICORN

EASY

Finished Size: 24" wide x 26" high (61 cm x 66 cm)

SHOPPING LIST

Yarn (Medium Weight)

[7 ounces, 426 yards (197 grams, 389 meters) per skein]:

- ☐ White - 2 skeins
- ☐ Purple - 30 yards (27.5 meters)
- ☐ Blue - 30 yards (27.5 meters)
- ☐ Yellow - 12 yards (11 meters)
- ☐ Pink - 12 yards (11 meters)
- ☐ Black - 10 yards (9 meters)

Crochet Hook

- ☐ Size J (6 mm) **or** size needed for gauge

Additional Supplies

- ☐ Yarn needle

GAUGE INFORMATION

11 dc = 4" (10 cm);
6 rows = 3½" (9 cm)

Gauge Swatch:
15" wide x 2" high
(38 cm x 5 cm)

Work same as Muzzle on page 36 through Rnd 2: 87 dc.

STITCH GUIDE

DOUBLE CROCHET 2 TOGETHER ***(abbreviated dc2tog)*** (uses next 2 dc)

★ YO, insert hook in **next** dc, YO and pull up a loop, YO and draw through 2 loops on hook; repeat from ★ once **more**, YO and draw through all 3 loops on hook **(counts as one dc)**.

MUZZLE

With White, ch 40.

Rnd 1 (Right side)**:** Sc in second ch from hook and in each ch across to last ch, 3 sc in last ch; working in free loops of beginning ch ***(Fig. 2b, page 43)***, sc in each ch across to ch at base of first sc, 3 sc in next ch; join with slip st to first sc: 81 sc.

Note: Loop a short piece of yarn around any stitch to mark Rnd 1 as **right** side.

Rnd 2: Ch 2 (**does not count as a st, now and throughout**), dc in same st as joining and in next 37 sc, 2 dc in each of next 3 sc, dc in next sc and in each sc across to last 3 sc, 2 dc in each of last 3 sc; join with slip st to first dc: 87 dc.

Rnd 3: Ch 2, dc in same st as joining and in next 38 dc, 2 dc in next dc, (dc in next dc, 2 dc in next dc) twice, dc in next 38 dc, 2 dc in next dc, (dc in next dc, 2 dc in next dc) twice; join with slip st to first dc: 93 dc.

Rnd 4: Ch 2, dc in same st as joining and in next 37 dc, 2 dc in next dc, (dc in next 2 dc, 2 dc in next dc) twice, dc in next 39 dc, (2 dc in next dc, dc in next 2 dc) 3 times; join with slip st to first dc: 99 dc.

Rnd 5: Ch 2, dc in same st as joining and in next 37 dc, 2 dc in next dc, (dc in next 3 dc, 2 dc in next dc) twice, dc in next 40 dc, (2 dc in next dc, dc in next 3 dc) 3 times; join with slip st to first dc: 105 dc.

Rnd 6: Ch 2, dc in same st as joining and in next 41 dc, 2 dc in next dc, (dc in next 4 dc, 2 dc in next dc) twice, dc in next 41 dc, 2 dc in next dc, (dc in next 4 dc, 2 dc in next dc) twice; join with slip st to first dc: 111 dc.

Rnd 7: Ch 2, dc in same st as joining and in next 42 dc, 2 dc in next dc, (dc in next 5 dc, 2 dc in next dc) twice, dc in next 42 dc, 2 dc in next dc, (dc in next 5 dc, 2 dc in next dc) twice; join with slip st to first dc: 117 dc.

Rnd 8: Ch 2, dc in same st as joining and in next 37 dc, (sc in next 6 dc, 2 sc in next dc) 3 times, dc in next 37 dc, (sc in next 6 dc, 2 sc in next dc) 3 times; join with slip st to first dc: 123 sts.

Rnd 9: Ch 2, dc in same st as joining and in next 37 dc, (2 sc in next sc, sc in next 7 sc) 3 times, dc in next 37 dc, (2 sc in next sc, sc in next 7 sc) 3 times; join with slip st to first dc: 129 sts.

Rnd 10: Ch 2, dc in same st as joining and in next 37 dc, 2 dc in next sc, (dc in next 8 sc, 2 dc in next sc) twice, dc in next 45 sts, (2 dc in next sc, dc in next 8 sc) 3 times; join with slip st to first dc: 135 dc.

Rnd 11: Ch 2, dc in same st as joining and in next 46 dc, 2 dc in next dc, (dc in next 9 dc, 2 dc in next dc) twice, dc in next 46 dc, 2 dc in next dc, (dc in next 9 dc, 2 dc in next dc) twice; join with slip st to first dc: 141 dc.

Rnd 12: Ch 2, dc in same st as joining and in next 47 dc, 2 dc in next dc, (dc in next 10 dc, 2 dc in next dc) twice, dc in next 47 dc, 2 dc in next dc, (dc in next 10 dc, 2 dc in next dc) twice; join with slip st to first dc: 147 dc.

Rnd 13: Ch 2, dc in same st as joining and in next 37 dc, 2 dc in next dc, (dc in next 11 dc, 2 dc in next dc) twice, dc in next 48 dc, (2 dc in next dc, dc in next 11 dc) 3 times; join with slip st to first dc, do **not** finish off: 153 dc.

HEAD

Row 1: Ch 3 **(counts as first dc, now and throughout)**, dc in next 41 dc, leave remaining dc unworked: 42 dc.

Rows 2-8: Ch 3, turn; dc in next dc and in each dc across.

Rows 9-14: Ch 3, turn; dc2tog, dc in next dc and in each dc across to last 3 dc, dc2tog, dc in last dc: 30 dc.

Trim: Ch 1, turn; sc evenly around entire piece; join with slip st to first sc, finish off.

EAR (Make 2)

Row 1: With White, ch 2, sc in second ch from hook: one sc.

Row 2 (Right side)**:** Ch 1, turn; 3 sc in sc.

Note: Mark Row 2 as **right** side.

Row 3: Ch 1, turn; 2 sc in first sc, sc in next sc, 2 sc in last sc: 5 sc.

Row 4: Ch 1, turn; 2 sc in first sc, sc in next 3 sc, 2 sc in last sc: 7 sc.

Row 5: Ch 1, turn; 2 sc in first sc, sc in next 5 sc, 2 sc in last sc: 9 sc.

Rows 6-14: Ch 1, turn; sc in each sc across.

Trim: Ch 1, do **not** turn; sc in end of each row across, (sc, ch 1, sc) in free loop of beginning ch, sc in end of each row across, leave remaining sc unworked; finish off leaving a long end for sewing.

Using photo as a guide for placement and long ends, sew Ears to Head.

EDGING

With **right** side facing and working from **left** to **right**, join Purple with slip st in sc at inside edge of left Ear; ch 1, work reverse sc evenly around to inside edge of right Ear working 3 reverse sc in ch-1 sp of each Ear ***(Figs. 5a-d, page 45)***, leave sc at top of Head between Ears unworked; finish off.

HORN

Rows 1-3: With Yellow, work same as Ear: 5 sc.

Rows 4-18: Ch 1, turn; sc in each sc across.

Trim: Ch 1, do **not** turn; sc in end of each row across, (sc, ch 1, sc) in free loop of beginning ch, sc in end of each row across, slip st in first st on Row 18, leave remaining sc unworked; finish off leaving a long end for sewing.

EYE (Make 2)

Rnd 1 (Right side)**:** With White, ch 2, 8 sc in second ch from hook; join with slip st to first sc.

Note: Mark Rnd 1 as **right** side.

Rnd 2: Ch 1, 2 sc in same st as joining and in each sc around; join with slip st to first sc: 16 sc.

Rnd 3: Ch 1, sc in same st as joining, 2 sc in next sc, (sc in next sc, 2 sc in next sc) around; join with slip st to first sc, finish off leaving a long end for sewing.

IRIS (Make 2)

Rnd 1 (Right side)**:** With Blue, ch 2, 8 sc in second ch from hook; join with slip st to first sc.

Note: Mark Rnd 1 as **right** side.

Rnd 2: Ch 1, 2 sc in same st as joining and in each sc around; join with slip st to first sc, finish off leaving a long end for sewing.

PUPIL (Make 2)

Rnd 1 (Right side)**:** With Black, ch 2, 8 sc in second ch from hook; join with slip st to first sc, finish off leaving a long end for sewing.

Note: Mark Rnd 1 as **right** side.

NOSTRIL (Make 2)

With Black, ch 4.

Rnd 1 (Right side)**:** Sc in second ch from hook, hdc in next ch, 3 dc in last ch; working in free loops of beginning ch, hdc in next ch, sc in next ch; join with slip st to first sc, finish off leaving a long end for sewing.

Note: Mark Rnd 1 as **right** side.

MOUTH

With Black, ch 16; finish off leaving a long end for sewing.

FINISHING

Using photo on page 39 as a guide for placement, with **right** sides of all pieces facing and using long ends:
Sew Pupils to Irises, then sew Irises to Eyes. Using satin stitch ***(Figs. 8a & b, page 47)***, add White to each Eye.
Sew Eyes to Head.
Sew Horn to Head.
Sew Nostrils and Mouth to Muzzle.

BANGS

Cut approximately 25 strands of Pink, Yellow, Blue, **and** Purple, each 14" (35.5 cm) long. Using photo as a guide for placement, fold two strands in half. With **wrong** side facing and using a crochet hook, draw the folded end up through unworked sc on Trim and pull the loose ends through the folded end ***(Fig. A)***; draw the knot up tightly ***(Fig. B)***. Repeat across the Head and in front of the Ears.

Fig. A

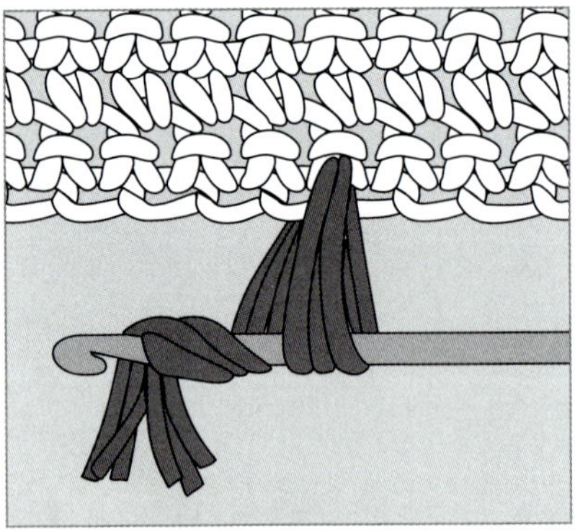

Fig. B

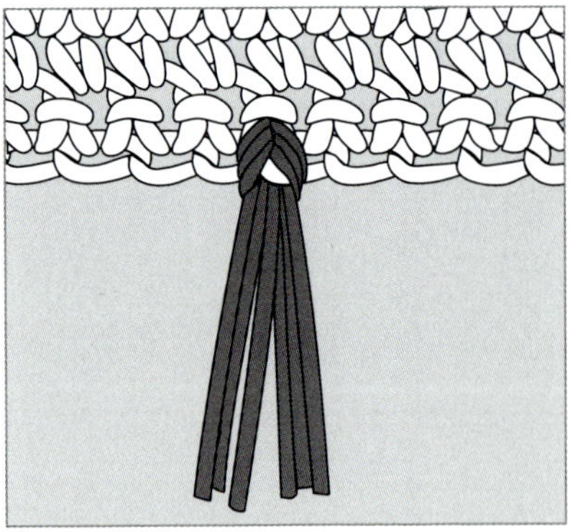

GENERAL INSTRUCTIONS

ABBREVIATIONS

ch(s)	chain(s)
cm	centimeters
dc	double crochet(s)
dc2tog	double crochet 2 together
hdc	half double crochet(s)
mm	millimeters
Rnd(s)	Round(s)
sc	single crochet(s)
sc2tog	single crochet 2 together
sp(s)	space(s)
st(s)	stitch(es)
tr	treble crochet(s)
YO	yarn over

CROCHET TERMINOLOGY		
UNITED STATES		INTERNATIONAL
slip stitch (slip st)	=	single crochet (sc)
single crochet (sc)	=	double crochet (dc)
half double crochet (hdc)	=	half treble crochet (htr)
double crochet (dc)	=	treble crochet (tr)
treble crochet (tr)	=	double treble crochet (dtr)
double treble crochet (dtr)	=	triple treble crochet (ttr)
triple treble crochet (tr tr)	=	quadruple treble crochet (qtr)
skip	=	miss

SYMBOLS & TERMS

★ — work instructions following ★ as many **more** times as indicated in addition to the first time.

† to † — work all instructions from first † to second † **as many** times as specified.

( ) or **[ ]** — work enclosed instructions **as many** times as specified by the number immediately following **or** work all enclosed instructions in the stitch or space indicated **or** contains explanatory remarks.

colon (:) — the number(s) given after a colon at the end of a row or round denote(s) the number of stitches or spaces you should have on that row or round.

BEGINNER	Projects for first-time crocheters using basic stitches. Minimal shaping.
EASY	Projects using yarn with basic stitches, repetitive stitch patterns, simple color changes, and simple shaping and finishing.
INTERMEDIATE	Projects using a variety of techniques, such as basic lace patterns or color patterns, mid-level shaping and finishing.
EXPERIENCED	Projects with intricate stitch patterns, techniques and dimension, such as non-repeating patterns, multi-color techniques, fine threads, small hooks, detailed shaping and refined finishing.

GAUGE

Exact gauge is **essential** for proper size. Before beginning your project, make the sample swatch given in the individual instructions in the yarn and hook specified. After completing the swatch, measure it, counting your stitches and rows carefully. If your swatch is larger or smaller than specified, **make another, changing hook size to get the correct gauge**. Keep trying until you find the size hook that will give you the specified gauge.

JOINING WITH SC

When instructed to join with sc, begin with a slip knot on hook. Insert hook in stitch or space indicated, YO and pull up a loop, YO and draw through both loops on hook.

JOINING WITH DC

When instructed to join with dc, begin with a slip knot on hook. YO, holding loop on hook, insert hook in space indicated, YO and pull up a loop (3 loops on hook), (YO and draw through 2 loops on hook) twice.

Yarn Weight Symbol & Names	LACE 0	SUPER FINE 1	FINE 2	LIGHT 3	MEDIUM 4	BULKY 5	SUPER BULKY 6	JUMBO 7
Type of Yarns in Category	Fingering, size 10 crochet thread	Sock, Fingering, Baby	Sport, Baby	DK, Light Worsted	Worsted, Afghan, Aran	Chunky, Craft, Rug	Super Bulky, Roving	Jumbo, Roving
Crochet Gauge* Ranges in Single Crochet to 4" (10 cm)	32-42 sts**	21-32 sts	16-20 sts	12-17 sts	11-14 sts	8-11 sts	6-9 sts	5 sts and fewer
Advised Hook Size Range	Steel*** 6 to 8, Regular hook B-1	B-1 to E-4	E-4 to 7	7 to I-9	I-9 to K-10½	K-10½ to M/N-13	M/N-13 to Q	Q and larger

*GUIDELINES ONLY: The chart above reflects the most commonly used gauges and hook sizes for specific yarn categories.

** Lace weight yarns are usually crocheted with larger hooks to create lacy openwork patterns. Accordingly, a gauge range is difficult to determine. Always follow the gauge stated in your pattern.

*** Steel crochet hooks are sized differently from regular hooks–the higher the number, the smaller the hook, which is the reverse of regular hook sizing.

BACK RIDGE OF A CHAIN

Work only in loops indicated by arrows *(Fig. 1)*.

Fig. 1

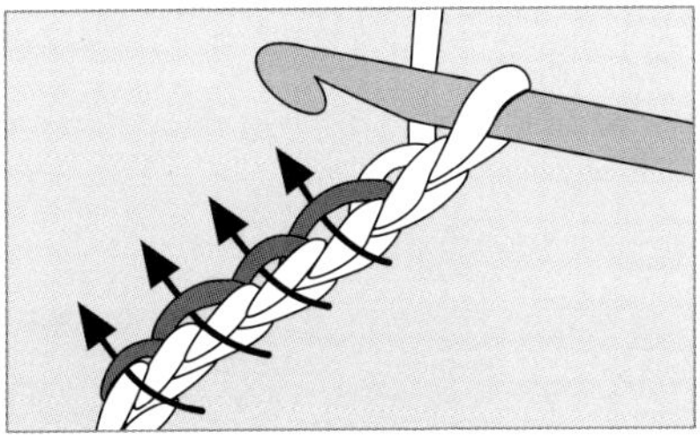

CROCHET HOOKS	
U.S.	Metric mm
B-1	2.25
C-2	2.75
D-3	3.25
E-4	3.5
F-5	3.75
G-6	4
7	4.5
H-8	5
I-9	5.5
J-10	6
K-10½	6.5
L-11	8
M/N-13	9
N/P-15	10
P/Q	15
Q	16
S	19

FREE LOOPS

After working in Back or Front Loops Only on a row or round, there will be a ridge of unused loops. These are called the free loops. Later, when instructed to work in the free loops of the same row or round, work in these loops *(Fig. 2a)*.

When instructed to work in free loops of a chain, work in loop indicated by arrow *(Fig. 2b)*.

Fig. 2a

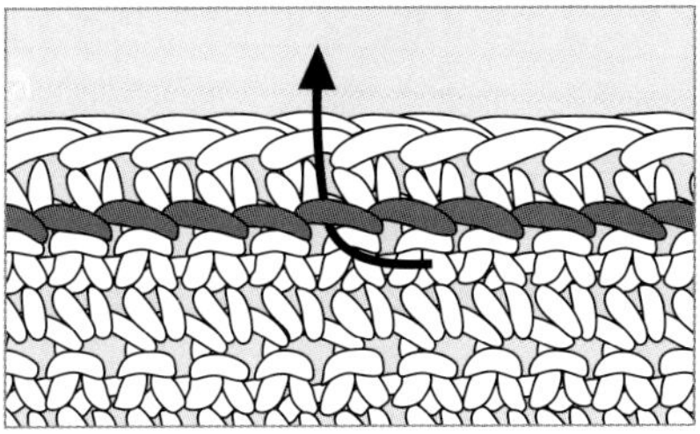

Fig. 2b

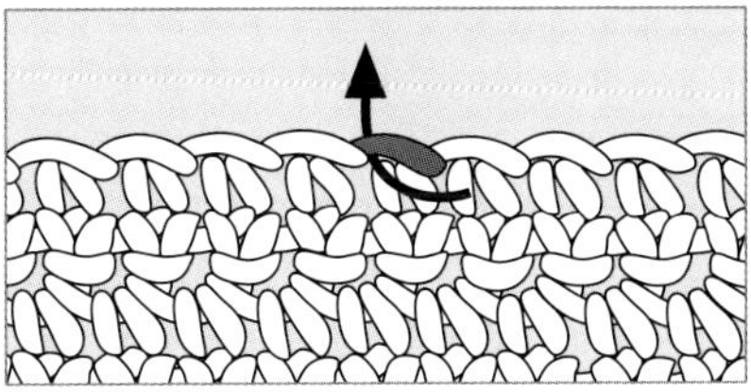

WORKING IN A SPACE BEFORE A STITCH

When instructed to work in a space **before** a stitch or in spaces **between** stitches, insert hook in space indicated by arrow ***(Fig. 3)***.

Fig. 3

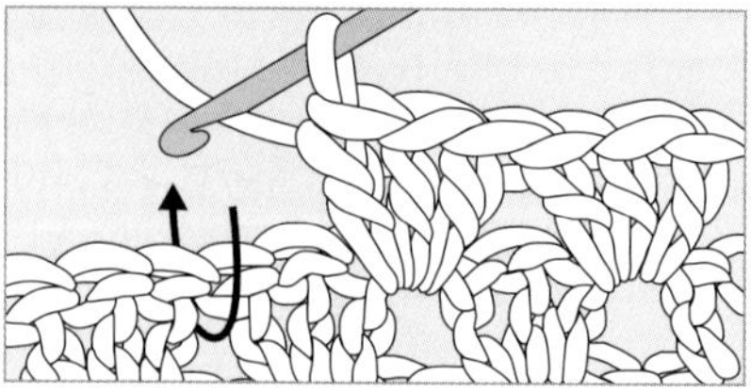

MATTRESS STITCH
(abbreviated Mattress St)

Hold 2 Motifs or Squares side-by-side with **right** sides facing. Thread yarn needle with yarn and sew pieces together ***(Figs. 4a & b)***.

Fig. 4a

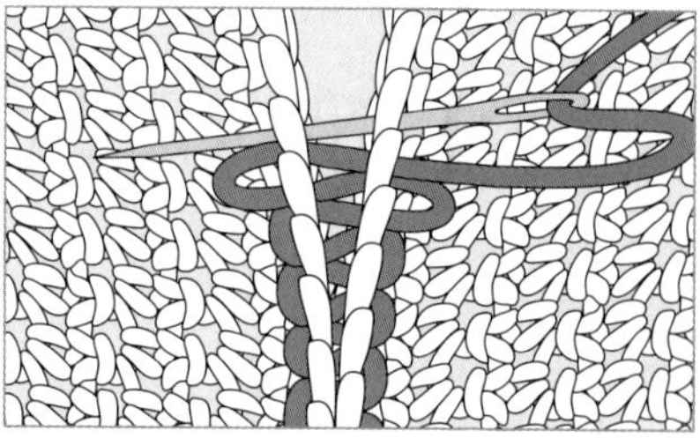

Fig. 4b

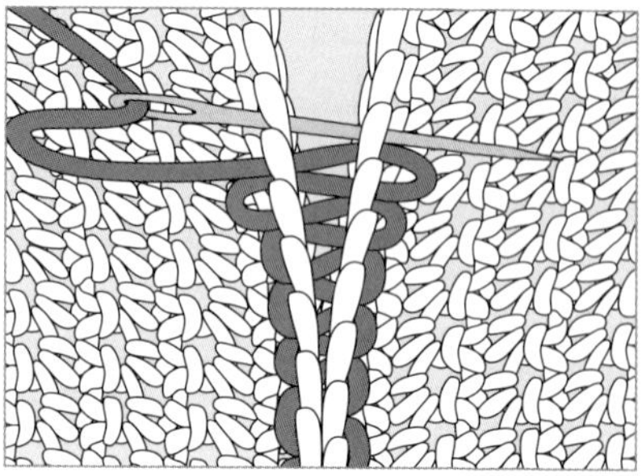

REVERSE SINGLE CROCHET
(abbreviated reverse sc)

Working from **left** to **right**, ★ insert hook in st to right of hook ***(Fig. 5a)***, YO and draw through, under and to left of loop on hook (2 loops on hook) ***(Fig. 5b)***, YO and draw through both loops on hook ***(Fig. 5c)*** **(reverse sc made, *Fig. 5d*)**; repeat from ★ as instructed.

Fig. 5a

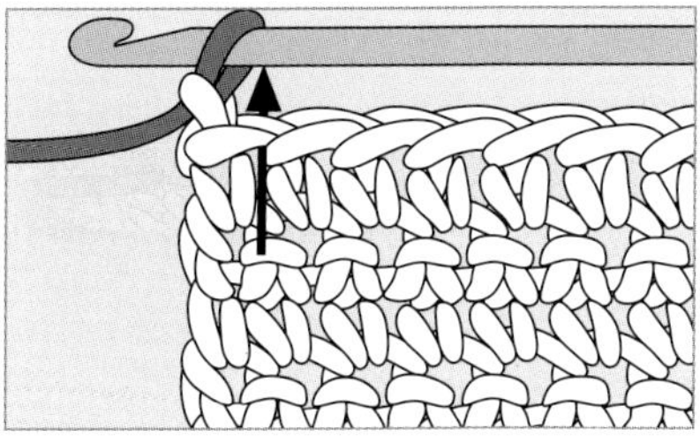

Fig. 5b

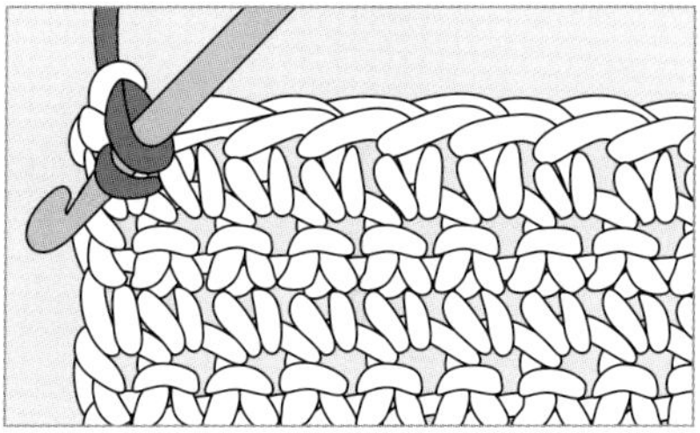

Fig. 5c

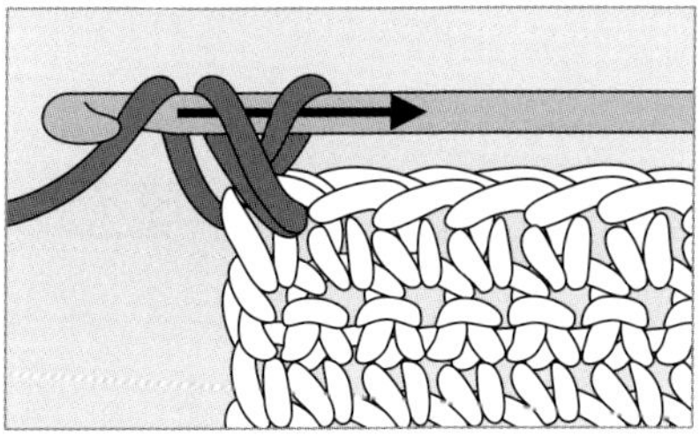

Fig. 5d

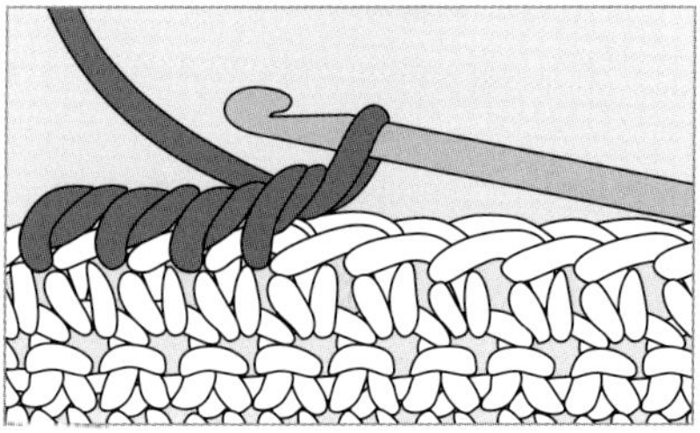

EMBROIDERY STITCHES

BACKSTITCH

The backstitch is worked from **right** to **left**. Come up at 1, go down at 2 and come up at 3 ***(Fig. 6)***. The second stitch is made by going down at 1 and coming up at 4.

Fig. 6

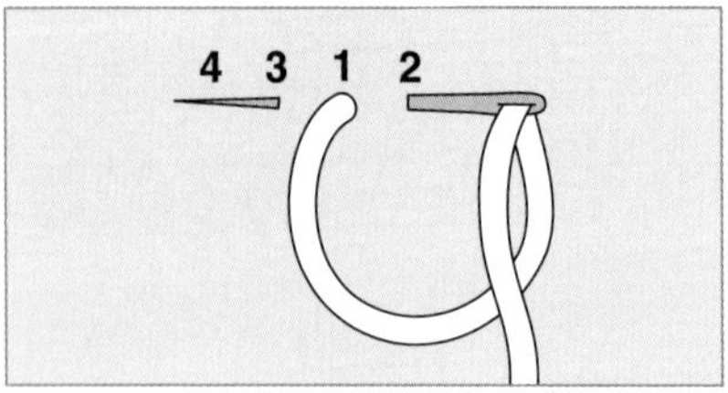

STRAIGHT STITCH

Straight stitch is just what the name implies, a single, straight stitch. Come up at 1 and go down at 2 ***(Fig. 7)***.

Fig. 7

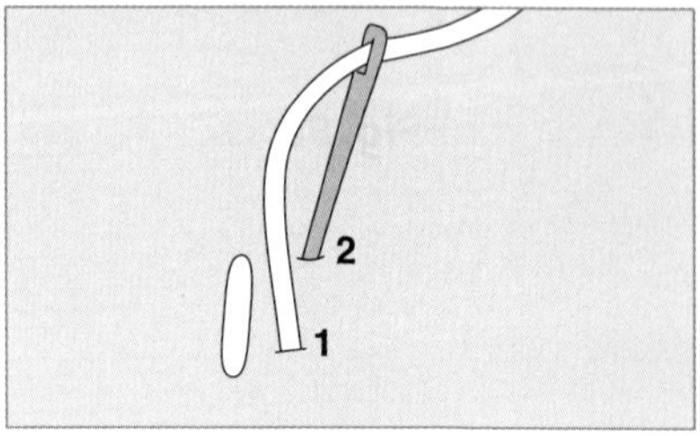

SATIN STITCH

Satin stitch is a series of straight stitches worked side by side that touch but do not overlap ***(Fig. 8a)*** **or** come out of and go into the same stitch ***(Fig. 8b)***. Come up at odd numbers and go down at even numbers.

Fig. 8a

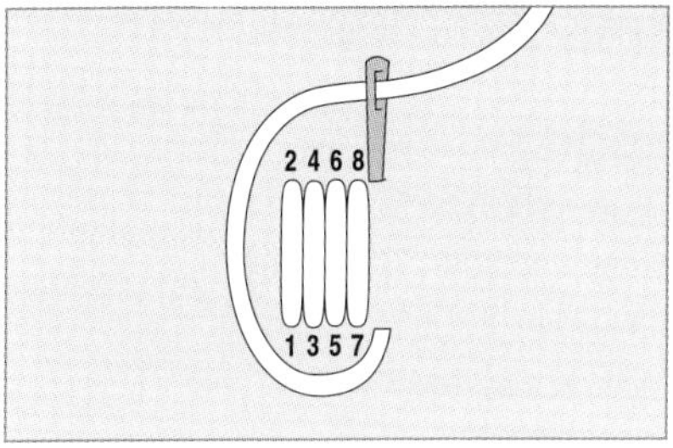

Fig. 8b

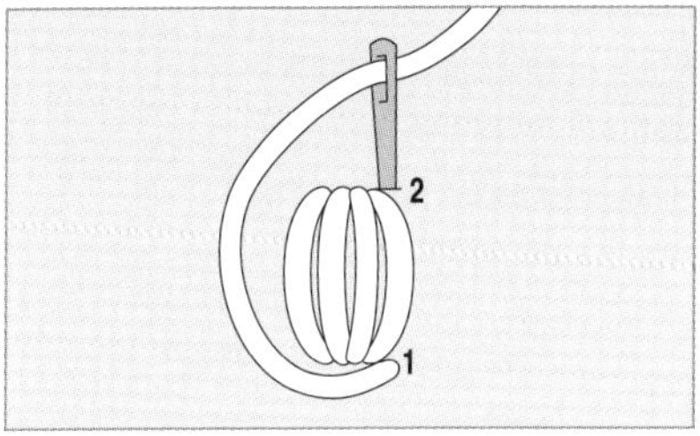

RUNNING STITCH

Running stitch is a series of straight stitches that weave in and out of the fabric. Come up at 1, go down at 2, come up at 3, and go down at 4 ***(Fig. 9)***. Continue in the same manner.

Fig. 9

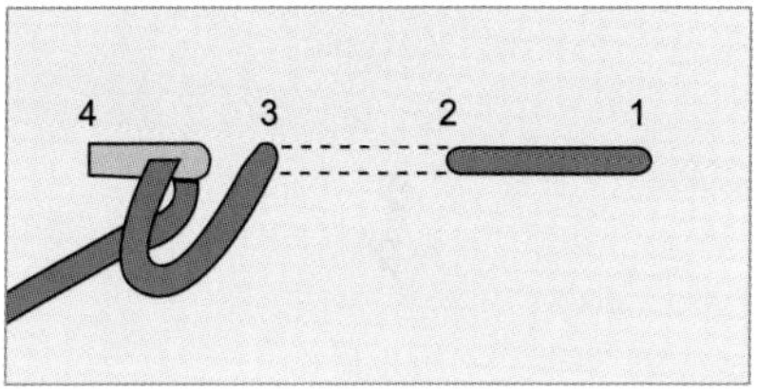

YARN INFORMATION

The Rugs in this book were made using Bernat® Super Value™, a Medium Weight yarn. Any brand of the specified yarn weight may be used. It is best to refer to the yardage/meters when determining how many balls or skeins to purchase. Remember, to arrive at the finished size, it is the GAUGE/TENSION that is important, not the brand of yarn.

For your convenience, listed below are the specific colors used to create our photography models. Because yarn manufacturers make frequent changes in their product lines, you may sometimes find it necessary to use a substitute yarn or to search for the discontinued product at alternate suppliers (locally or online).

OWL
Ecru - #07414 Natural
Grey - #53046 Soft Grey
Rose - #53402 Magenta

COW
White - #07391White
Pink - #07438 Baby Pink
Black - #07421 Black

PENGUIN
White - #07391 White
Black - #07421 Black
Orange - #00615 Carrot

RACETRACK
Green - #53223 Grass
Black - #07421 Black
Blue - #08879 Sky
Yellow - #07445 Yellow

ROCKET
Blue - #08879 Sky
Grey - #53044 True Grey
Orange - #00615 Carrot
Yellow - #07445 Yellow

UNICORN
White - #07391 White
Purple - #53333 Mulberry
Blue - #00616 Peacock
Yellow - #07445 Yellow
Pink - #53417 Peony Pink
Black - #07421 Black

We have made every effort to ensure that these instructions are accurate and complete. We cannot, however, be responsible for human error, typographical mistakes, or variations in individual work.

Production Team: Instructional/Technical Writer - Lois J. Long; Editorial Writer - Susan Frantz Wiles; Senior Graphic Artist - Lora Puls; Photo Stylist - Stephanie Moore; and Photographer - Jason Masters.

Copyright © 2018 by Leisure Arts, Inc., 104 Champs Blvd., STE 100, Maumelle, AR 72113-6738, www.leisurearts.com. All rights reserved. This publication is protected under federal copyright laws. Reproduction or distribution of this publication or any other Leisure Arts publication, including publications which are out of print, is prohibited unless specifically authorized. This includes, but is not limited to, any form of reproduction or distribution on or through the Internet, including posting, scanning, or e-mail transmission.

